Donated by
Roswell
Rotary Club
2011

LIFE SKILLS

PANIC-FREE PRESENTATIONS

Greg Paulk
with Elisa Paulk

CRABAPPLE
MIDDLE SCHOOL
MEDIA CENTER

Heinemann Library
Chicago, Illinois

808.5
PAU

Customer Service 888-454-2279

Visit our website at www.heinemannraintree.com

Editorial: Megan Cotugno and Harriet Milles
Design: Philippa Jenkins
Production: Alison Parsons
Picture Research: Liz Alexander
Originated by Chroma Graphics (Overseas) Pte. Ltd
Printed and bound in China by South China Printing Company Ltd.

13 12 11 10 09
10 9 8 7 6 5 4 3 2 1

Library of Congress Cataloging-in-Publication Data
Paulk, Greg.
  Panic-free presentations / Greg Paulk with Elisa Paulk. -- 1st ed.
     p. cm. -- (Life skills)
  Includes bibliographical references and index.
  ISBN 978-1-4329-1355-7 (hc)
  1. Public speaking. 2. Speech--Physiological aspects. I. Paulk, Elisa. II. Title.
  PN4129.15.P38 2008
  808.5'1--dc22
                        2008020151

Acknowledgments
The author and publisher are grateful to the following for permission to reproduce copyright material:
©Alamy **pp. 8** (Frances Roberts), **5** (Michael Doolittle); ©Corbis/Bettmann **pp. 21, 23, 28, 13**; ©Corbis **pp. 47** (Randy Faris), **26** (Reuters), **41** (Rob Melnychuk/Brand X), **14** (Thinkstock); ©Getty Images **pp. 39** (Bridgeman Art Library), **27** (Jurgen Schadeberg), **18** (Photographer's Choice/Frederic Tousche), **31** (The Image Bank/Colin Hawkins), **48** (The Image Bank/Yellow Dog Productions), **29** (Time & Life Pictures/Mansell), **24** (AFP Photo/Nicholas Roberts); ©Istockphoto/Oleg Prikhodko **p. 32**; ©Pearson Education Ltd. **p. 43**; ©Photolibrary/Nonstock **p. 37**; ©Rex Features **pp. 17** (Dave Allocca), **7** (Everett Collection); ©Topham Picturepoint/Jeff Greenberg/The Image Works **p. 11**.

Cover photograph of boy in a panic reproduced with permission of ©2008 Masterfile Corporation/Edward Pond. Photograph of microphones with permission of ©istockphoto / Krzysztof Kwiatkowski.

The publisher would like to thank Tristan Boyer Binns for her invaluable assistance in the preparation of this book.

Every effort has been made to contact copyright holders of any material reproduced in this book. Any omissions will be rectified in subsequent printings if notice is given to the publisher.

Contents

Some words are printed in bold, **like this**. You can find out what they mean by looking in the glossary.

686019140

Taking The Panic Out Of Presentations

Imagine that you're about to deliver an important presentation in front of the entire school. Scared? Well help is at hand! The purpose of this book is to make you realize that giving presentations can be a breeze. All you need is passion for your subject—and preparation, preparation, preparation.

WHY WORK ON PUBLIC SPEAKING?

One of the most common fears people have is public speaking. A large percentage of adults are terrified of speaking in front of a crowd.

At some point in your life *you* are almost bound to be asked to speak in public for some reason. You might be asked to make a presentation in front of a class for an assignment; or speak in front of the school to run for student council president.

Right now you are only imagining yourself in that situation, but chances are, it will happen at some point in the future. It might be next week, or it might be years from now.

Questions to ask yourself

Are you confident that you will know your topic and be able to deliver your speech smoothly? If your audience asks you questions about your topic, will you have all your answers thoroughly prepared?

How you answer these questions will have a lot to do with how well your presentation goes.

Don't panic—prepare!

The main reason people find public speaking frightening is that they often haven't prepared their speech properly—or they don't know how to write and deliver a great speech or presentation. This book is designed to teach you a few simple techniques that will help you deliver a memorable speech. It will give you the tools you need to help you to choose a topic, calm your nerves on the big day, and hold your audience's interest.

Just remember not to panic—public speaking is a skill that you can learn like any other, and it gets easier with practice. With solid preparation and a few helpful tips, making a presentation doesn't have to be scary. It is even possible to enjoy it!

By the time you have finished reading this book you will have learned some basic facts about:

- How to research your topic
- How to write your speech
- How to calm your nerves

- How to stand properly
- How to use your voice effectively
- How to handle props and **visuals**
- How to use **eye contac**t
- How to use gestures
- How to dress
- How to breathe!

So, read on and prepare to deliver a panic-free presentation!

"There are three things to aim at in public speaking: first, to get into your subject, then to get your subject into yourself, and lastly, to get your subject into the heart of your audience."

–Alexander Gregg (1819-1893)

Clergyman and the first Bishop of Texas

Most people get nervous before a presentation. But if you have prepared properly, you will feel more confident.

Preparing For A Presentation

The first step in making a presentation is deciding what you're going to talk about. Speakers may or may not have control over this part of the presentation. A speech may be on an assigned subject, or you may be free to choose your own topic.

Great Speeches

Most of the great speeches from history are great because the speaker really believed in what he or she was talking about. Some people are simply wonderful speakers, whatever the topic. But anyone can give a great presentation if they understand their topic and have enthusiasm for it. Sharing that enthusiasm with your audience is the key to a great presentation. At the end of your presentation, they may not know as much as you do about the subject, but they should have a strong feeling about it, and a willingness to explore it further.

Caring and sharing

Dull presentations usually happen when the speaker doesn't care about the topic. Audiences are sensitive and smart—they know when someone is filling time, and they dislike having their time wasted.

Think about the best speeches you've ever heard in your lifetime. What made those speeches memorable? Was it the speaker's attitude or performance, the words he or she delivered, or both? It might also be helpful to think about some bad speeches you've heard. What, if anything, did those poor presentations have in common?

You can learn a lot just from listening carefully to other presentations and noting what worked and what didn't work about them.

Choosing your topic

If you are selecting a topic to speak about, think about your likes and dislikes. What are you interested in? What makes you angry or frustrated?

If you are given a list of topics to choose from, make sure you sign up early to find a subject you will enjoy. If your instructor assigns you a topic that you know nothing about, make sure you do your research. Develop an opinion. Become an expert. Before your presentation, make sure you get a strong feeling about your topic.

MARTIN LUTHER KING JR.

Martin Luther King Jr. spent his adult life campaigning for equal rights for African-Americans. In 1963, he gave an excellent speech at a huge civil rights rally in Washington, D.C. He had a commanding manner while he spoke, but what made people listen was the fact that he was talking about something in which he passionately believed.

"I have a dream that one day this nation will rise up and live out the true meaning of its creed: "… that all men are created equal."

I have a dream that one day … the sons of former slaves and the sons of former slave owners will be able to sit down together at the table of brotherhood. …

I have a dream that my four little children will one day live in a nation where they will not be judged by the color of their skin but by the content of their character.

I have a dream today."

August 28, 1963

FINDING A STUDY SPOT

When researching and preparing for a presentation, you will need to find the right study spot. This space should be quiet enough so you can focus on your research and writing, but it also should allow you to make some noise. After all, you will need to practice reading lines of your speech out loud. It's not always possible to find a place where you can do both, so you may have to find a place to practice as well.

Next, make sure you have all the materials you need to prepare. Notebooks, paper, pens, pencils, highlighters—anything you like to use when doing research. Most speakers use index cards for notes while talking. Many use computer slide presentations too. It will help you do better work if you have access to a library and a computer.

If you leave your planning to the last minute, you are likely to panic and it will be hard to concentrate.

Getting it Wrong

Never leave your preparation until the night before your presentation. Leaving things to the last minute is called **procrastination**. It can mean the difference between a great speech and one that just barely makes the grade, or even fails. By giving yourself time to prepare and practice, you can give your presentation with confidence. Confidence gives you **conviction**. Conviction makes your audience believe in you, and believe in what you are telling them.

TEST YOUR PROGRESS

1) **Which of the following questions should you *not* ask when learning about your topic?**
   a) How in depth should it be?
   b) How long can the presentation be?
   c) Can I use visual props?
   d) Can I be excused from doing this assignment?

2) **When finding a place to study, you should look for a place that:**
   a) Is loud and exciting, to stop you getting bored
   b) Is quiet, but doesn't require you to be completely silent
   c) Doesn't permit you to speak
   d) Serves food.

3) **Which of the following materials are not necessary for preparing a speech?**
   a) A notebook with lots of paper.
   b) Pencils, pens, and highlighters.
   c) Access to a computer and library.
   d) An iPod, a Gameboy, and a TV.

Check page 50 to check your answers.

Researching Your Topic

To put together a presentation that will keep your audience attentive and entertained, you will first need to learn as much as possible about your topic. The more you know about your topic, the more confident you will be when speaking about it. The more confidence you have, the more relaxed you will be.

Researching with a Questionnaire

Filling out a questionnaire is a good way to get started researching your topic. Ask yourself some basic questions about your topic and make notes similar to the example shown on the checklist on page 11. An especially good question is "Why is this an important topic?" You need to find out as much background information about the topic as you can. A firm grasp of the basics will allow you to delve deeper into the topic later and discover new insights.

Ask around

Ask everyone you can what they know about your topic. Use the same questions that you ask yourself. Not every response will be helpful, but many will point to new ideas. Ask your teachers, parents, and friends. Maybe someone will know an expert in the field. This is one of the easiest parts of researching, but it is often the most overlooked.

Getting it Wrong

Don't try to learn only the bare minimum about your topic. You'll never feel confident, and it will show when you're speaking.

Don't think you'll remember everything you research without writing it down in an organized manner. Taking notes is a vital part of research.

Don't get your notes so mixed up that you can't read them. Make sure your notes are organized. Index cards help, as does typing notes into a document that can be cut and pasted into order.

Using a questionnaire to gather opinions from people can give you fresh ideas and different viewpoints.

→

• CHECKLIST •

RESEARCHING THE AZTEC EMPIRE

1. What do I know about this topic?
   - The heart of the Aztec Empire was Tenochtitlan.
   - Tenochtitlan is now Mexico City.
   - The Aztec Empire was located in present-day Mexico.

2. What do I need to learn about this topic?
   - When did the Aztec Empire exist?
   - What important contributions did the Aztec Empire make?
   - What happened to the Aztec Empire?
   - What was the culture like?

3. Why is this an important topic?
   - Because the Aztecs helped create the modern calendar
   - Because they shaped the culture and history of Mexico and parts of the United States.

4. How can I make this topic immediately interesting to my audience?
   - I can begin with an arresting fact—like the human sacrifices Aztecs used to make. They even sacrificed butterflies!

Good research

Once you have chosen your topics ask yourself the following questions:

- What do you know?
- What do you need to learn?
- Who is affected?
- How are they affected?
- Why is this important?

Use what you know

Write down what you already know about your topic. Even the smallest bit will help you in your research. What *don't* you know about this issue? The topic will bring to mind many questions—write them down. Who is affected by this issue? How might they be affected? This is a good way to focus or direct your research.

Lastly, why is this issue important? If you can't tell your audience why this issue is important, it's going to be hard to keep their attention.

Online research

The easiest way to start researching your topic on the Internet is to open a search engine such as Yahoo, Google, or Dogpile and type in the exact wording of your topic. You will be amazed at how many hits you will get without refining your search.

With a little experience, you will discover which sites tend to be the best. Commercial sites—or sites run by companies—are usually very one sided because they are trying to sell you something. Web logs or blogs are not usually a good source of facts, but they can be a good way to find links to actual data.

The table below will help you understand the function of some website domains.

Domain	Source	Purpose
.com	companies	product oriented
.org	organizations	usually noncommercial
.edu	educational institutions	educational
.gov	government	government websites

PRESIDENT JOHN F. KENNEDY

President John F. Kennedy gave a great speech in 1962 when he wanted to tell people why the US was aiming to put people on the Moon. He used facts and figures to paint a picture.

"No man can fully grasp how far and how fast we have come, but condense ... the past 50,000 years of man's recorded history in a time span of but a half-century [50 years]. ... we know very little about the first 40 years, except at the end of them advanced man had learned to use the skins of animals to cover them. Then about 10 years ago ... man emerged from his caves to construct other kinds of shelter. Only five years ago man learned to write and use a cart with wheels. Christianity began less than two years ago. The printing press came this year, and then less than two months ago, ... the steam engine provided a new source of power. Last month electric lights and telephones and automobiles and airplanes became available. Only last week did we develop penicillin and television and nuclear power, and now if America's new spacecraft succeeds in reaching Venus, we will have literally reached the stars before midnight tonight.

...We choose to go to the Moon. We choose to go to the Moon in this decade and do the other things, not because they are easy, but because they are hard, ... because that challenge is one that we are willing to accept, one we are unwilling to postpone, and one which we intend to win ... ."

*From Kennedy's
"Address at Rice University
on the Nation's Space Effort,"
made on September 12, 1962.*

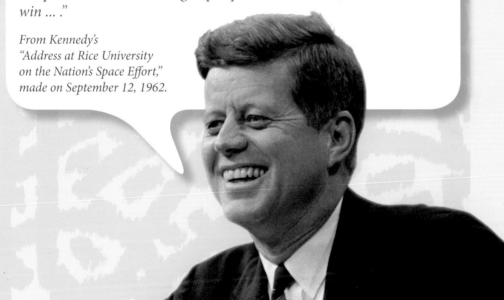

Library research

One of the best ways to find out about a topic is to ask a librarian. A library is a fantastic resource for students, and librarians can help you research any topic. Some librarians have been specially trained to carry out research. They can give you useful tips on how to structure your research and where to find the right in-depth information.

As well as a vast selection of books, most libraries also give you access to online references, such as dictionaries, biographies, and encyclopedias on specialized topics. They can usually borrow books from other library systems.

Getting it Right

To stay fully focused on your research, it is important to work in an environment that has no distractions. Do not try and research with the TV on or while talking on the phone, or you might skip over an important part of the research.

A librarian can help you find the information you need more quickly. They can also advise on other sources of information.

Choosing your words

It is a good idea to ask a teacher or someone familiar with your topic if there is any **specialized vocabulary** you might need to know. Using the correct vocabulary will make you sound like an expert.

Don't assume you can pronounce unfamiliar words just by sounding them out. Always check foreign or difficult words in a pronunciation guide, or ask an expert.

Be sure that you understand what special words or phrases mean —especially if they are in a foreign language. A simple example is a French expression that English-speaking people use too, *coup de grace* (pronounced "*koo duh grahs*"). It translates literally as "blow of mercy." However, it is usually used to describe a finishing stroke or a decisive event.

Don't use a foreign phrase because you think it sounds cool. If you really don't know what it means, or cannot pronounce it, you will simply sound **pretentious** and foolish—and not cool at all! You will feel much more confident if you are using words that you understand and can pronounce correctly. So choose and research your words carefully.

BEGINNING RESEARCH

1) Which of the following is *not* a good question to ask yourself when beginning research?
   a) What is for dinner?
   b) Who is affected?
   c) What do I need to learn?
   d) What do I already know?

2) What is an essential part of research?
   a) Using questionnaires
   b) Focusing and directing your research
   c) Asking a librarian for help
   d) None of the above

3) Librarians are:
   a) Scary
   b) People who don't know about books
   c) Fantastic resources for students
   d) People who live in libraries.

Check page 50 to check your answers.

Writing Your Speech

As you research your topic, you will gather pages of information. At some point, you may feel you know all there is to know about the topic. This is when you need to think about what you want to say. Who is going to listen to you? What does this audience already know about the topic? What else do they need to know for you to make your point?

Getting Your Ideas Across

One of the most important parts of your presentation is outside your control—it's your audience. If you know a little about your audience, then you can make a presentation that will move, convince, amuse, or inform them.

Think about your audience

For example, if you were going to address the **United Nations** on the topic of peacekeeping, you could assume the audience already knew a lot about the topic of sending troops into countries to stop wars. However, if you were going to talk to a group of six-year-olds on the same topic, you would be talking about a different kind of peacekeeping altogether. They would most likely assume you meant stopping playground fights, or keeping the peace between siblings.

What are you trying to say?

Imagine that you are writing a speech explaining the function of your local town government. First do some

• CHECKLIST •

Questions to ask about your town:

- What are the elected and nonelected offices (and what is the difference)?
- Who are the elected officials?
- How do they get elected?
- What do all of these people do?
- How can we citizens access their help when we need it?

online or library research. Then you might want to actually speak to a few people in your local town government to learn more. This is called first-hand research, and it can be very powerful. By meeting and talking to government officials yourself, you can speak with more authority about what they do.

Using a solid base of facts is one of the most important parts of a good speech. The Greek **philosopher** and playright Aristotle, who lived over 2000 years ago, said, "The arousing of **prejudice**, pity, anger, and similar emotions has nothing to do with the essential facts, but is merely a personal appeal to the man who is judging the case." This means you should give the hard facts first, then build up the audience's emotions afterward. So, always start by building a framework of facts before you move on to the wording of your speech.

Why should they listen?

Next, you need to find a strong title for your speech. You need to get the interest of your audience, and it's usually best to keep the title simple. Perhaps it could be as simple as "What can your government do for you?"

The topic "What can your government do for you?" will mean different things to different people. If your audience is a group of fellow students at school, you can pick through your research for the facts that are likely to interest them most.

New York City Mayor, Michael Bloomberg meets some local students.

Words on paper

Sometimes you will be given a set length for your presentation, but other times it will be up to you. Always take the time you need, but don't let yourself speak too long. Be effective. Don't tell your audience everything you know, just tell them what you need to in order to prove your argument or explain your point.

So begin writing your presentation speech by stating your reason for giving it. This is often in the title itself. Then move onto building your framework of facts. Try writing this as a five-paragraph essay. If you keep the speech simple, it will be successful.

One speechwriter, who helps company leaders write their speeches, has said, "Keep it short. Expose an idea, defend it and motivate the audience quickly, then get off the stage." (James L. Horton, 2005).

TIP

One rule to remember is: Tell the audience what you're going to tell them, tell it to them, then tell them what you told them. Sounds funny, but it works!

←

Make quick notes of your main ideas, and then work on the structure of your speech. Aim to keep it short and simple.

SPEECH FORMAT

Title: What can your local government do for you?

1. Introduction—Outline of your presentation

a. Opening statement—should be powerful and memorable. ("Your government can change the world you live in for the better—it is there to serve you and your neighbors and improve the life of all who live here.")

b. State why the audience should care about your speech. ("If you understand how your government works, you can make your voice, your needs, and your concerns heard.")

c. State what you are going to tell them. ("I will explain today what offices there are in our local government, and who works in them. I will tell you how to contact them, and what rights you have.")

d. Tell them what they will learn or be able to do afterward. ("When you have heard all I have to say, you will be able to understand your part in our government, and how you can use your power to make your voice count.")

2. First point—What the offices are and who does what (fact)

a. Supporting fact

b. Supporting fact

3. Second point—How to contact officials (fact)

a. Supporting fact

b. Supporting fact

4. Third point—Your rights and how to use them (fact)

a. Supporting fact

b. Supporting fact

5. Conclusion—state what you have said again

a. First point with first impact

b. Second point with second impact

c. Third point with third impact

d. Explain how your points show why the audience should care. ("You no longer need to feel powerless as you complain to people who cannot help make change happen.")

e. Concluding statement ("Now you are armed with the knowledge you need to make your voice heard. Go out and use it!")

USING LANGUAGE WELL

So now you have your framework of facts, and know what you need to say. Next you need to think about how to say it. Writing to be read silently is different from writing to be read aloud. Try going to the famous speeches featured in this book. Read one you are not familiar with silently. Now read it out loud. Now have a look at the back of the book and see if there is a weblink so you can listen to the speech as it was given. Some even have videos to show the speaker giving the speech.

What was different with each way of hearing the speech? Did you feel different when you read the words out loud? Was it different again when you heard the recording of the speech?

A good speech has a lot in common with poetry. The words should be well-chosen. They need to tell your facts, but they need to do it with rhythm and elegance. The length of sentences, pauses, and the way you speak need to be thought about. Whatever the subject, a well-written speech should be pleasing for the audience to listen to.

Getting it Right

Writing a speech is an art. A good speech has many elements to it, including:

- A good reason for giving it.
- A strong framework of facts.
- A pleasing pattern of language.
- Good length.

As a writer, you can make your audience want to listen carefully to your words because they sound good. Skilled speakers use tools such as **alliteration** and repetition to get their message across. Alliteration is using words with the same sounds, such as "struggle" and "strong" or "brave" and "beautiful." Repetition is repeating keywords and phrases.

PATRICK HENRY

Patrick Henry was an **American patriot** during the War of Independence in the 1770s. He spoke to convince the colony of Virginia to join in the revolt against Britain in the 1770s. He gave a long, passionate speech without notes. This is only possible if you believe firmly in your topic, and know it inside and out. He told his listeners the facts as he saw them, but he used very **emotive** language. His use of words—"chains clanking," "clash of arms," "we here idle"—helped to spur his audience into action.

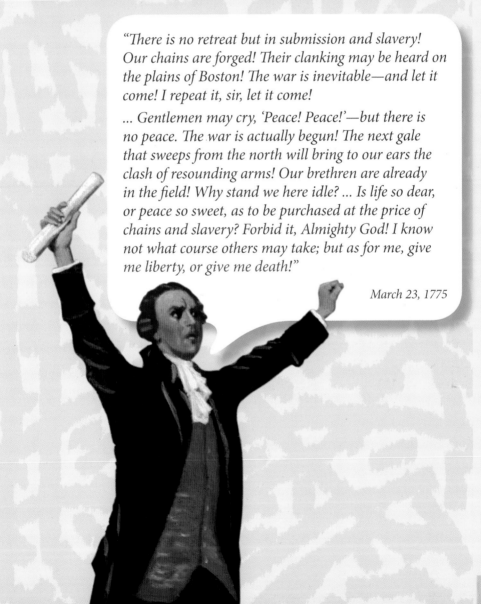

"There is no retreat but in submission and slavery! Our chains are forged! Their clanking may be heard on the plains of Boston! The war is inevitable—and let it come! I repeat it, sir, let it come!

... Gentlemen may cry, 'Peace! Peace!'—but there is no peace. The war is actually begun! The next gale that sweeps from the north will bring to our ears the clash of resounding arms! Our brethren are already in the field! Why stand we here idle? ... Is life so dear, or peace so sweet, as to be purchased at the price of chains and slavery? Forbid it, Almighty God! I know not what course others may take; but as for me, give me liberty, or give me death!"

March 23, 1775

• CHECKLIST •

Here are some tools to write a good speech:

- *Alliteration*—using the same sounds (*b*at, *b*all and *br*eakage; *s*mooth, *s*ilky, and *s*leek)

- *Varying length*—use short phrases to make a point, longer ones to draw an idea out ("You may say I can change no one's way of thinking with my words. You are wrong." "I came, I saw, I conquered" vs. "When I first arrived on the scene I took photos, wrote down what I heard and looked all around, then I decided which suspect to arrest.")

- *Word rhythm*—use words of different lengths too—long words make a different sound than short ones (*Incredible!* vs. *Wow!*, *television* vs. *TV*)

- *Interesting examples*—use thoughtful but unexpected ways to look at facts—could you talk about the size of a volcano's crater in terms of how many Olympic size swimming pools would fit in it? Or show how small germs are by saying how many would fit in the head of a pin?

Laying it out

Winston Churchill was the British prime minister during World War II. He was famously good at giving speeches. He wrote most of his own speeches, and he wrote many drafts. Each time he thought he had finished, he would reread his words, often out loud. Then he would work on the bits that still didn't satisfy him.

Some of the speeches he wrote by hand, but often he spoke them out loud to secretaries. He trained them to type his words in short phrases that moved in a slant across the page, so they looked like poems.

When Churchill read his speeches out, he paused at each line end. When he got to the end of a slanting passage, he knew it was time to begin a new idea. He could vary his tone and delivery of his speech by the way he laid them out.

WINSTON CHURCHILL

Winston Churchill knew he had to rally the support of the British people and lift their spirits when it looked possible that Germany might invade Britain during World War II. He couldn't lie and say things were going well, but he had to make them want to fight on and win. He used stirring language and repetition to drive his points home.

> "We shall go on to the end, we shall fight in France, we shall fight on the seas and oceans, we shall fight ... in the air, we shall defend our Island, whatever the cost may be, we shall fight on the beaches, we shall fight on the landing grounds, we shall fight in the fields and in the streets, we shall fight in the hills; we shall never surrender, and even if, which I do not for a moment believe, this Island ... were subjugated and starving, then our Empire beyond the seas, armed and guarded by the British Fleet, would carry on the struggle, until, in God's good time, the New World, with all its power and might, steps forth to the rescue and the liberation of the old."
>
> *June 4, 1940*

SCRIPTS AND NOTECARDS

The most effective way to give a speech is to have an office full of speechwriters and professionals writing your speech. You might also have a **teleprompter** in front of you scrolling through the speech at just the right speed. However, if you're not a national leader, you'll probably have to use a script or notecards.

You should first write out your speech as you intend to give it. Pass it around to a few trusted friends, adults, and teachers. Don't be discouraged by all of the comments they will make—you don't have to use all of them.

Now rewrite your speech until you have a solid final draft. Read it through several times until you are comfortable. Take notes from your speech so that you will remember what you need to say.

Now, throw away your speech. Yes, throw it away. If you stand up in front of a crowd with a written speech, guess what you are most likely going to do? Of course you'll read it—and fast, too! Nothing sounds worse, or more unnatural, than someone reading their speech off a sheet of paper, word for word. But if you only have notes, you can't read the speech.

Most politicians and public speakers use teleprompters for TV speeches or presentations. They want their audience to believe they are not using notes.

I SAY TO YOU TONIGHT: A NEW DAY IS ON THE WAY.

####

Making notes

Make note cards that state your main points. Leave off the details. You'll have to fill in the blanks with your own words. It will sound much better and will help keep your audience focused on what you are saying.

Don't wait until the last minute to get your notes together. It's best to practice as much as possible with the actual notes that you will use. If you are using notecards, make sure they are readable. You might want to use a marker to make them stand out. Keep them clear and simple.

Whatever notes you use, be sure to number them. If you don't, they may suddenly and mysteriously fall from your hands and scatter. This is where the numbering comes in handy. You could even punch a hole in them and keep them together with a short piece of string or ribbon.

*"It usually takes me more than three weeks to prepare a good **impromptu** speech."*

Mark Twain (1835-1910)
American humorist and writer

SPEECH DELIVERY

1) It is important to
 a) Have a purpose and be aware of your audience
 b) Have a dance routine
 c) Read your speech word for word
 d) Not practice

2) It is a good idea to
 a) Make pretty pictures on your notes
 b) Have no purpose to your speech, just get up there and say *"hi folks"*
 c) Give your audience a purpose for your presentation
 d) Not have an audience

3) If you are presenting to students, what should you be sure to do?
 a) Ask the right questions
 b) Pretend you're invisible
 c) Have a boring speech
 d) Don't prepare—just wing it

Check page 50 to check your answers.

WHY GIVE A SPEECH?

Most speeches try to convince the audience to think the way the speaker thinks. Sometimes people risk a lot—even their lives—for a cause in which they believe. Their speeches tell us why we should support their cause too. Here are four famous speeches, all talking about injustices that were once legal. Great changes have been made now, partly due to the work these people put into speaking about them.

PAUL KEATING

Injustice to the first Australians

Paul Keating was Australia's prime minister when he gave this speech in 1992 in Sydney. He spoke about the past unjust treatment toward the **indigenous** Aboriginal people by white Australians. He said that these injustices must never happen again.

"We took the [Aborigines'] traditional lands and smashed the traditional way of life. We brought the disasters. ...We committed the murders. We took the children from their mothers. We practiced **discrimination** and exclusion.

It was our ignorance and our prejudice. ... We failed to ask—how would I feel if this were done to me? As a consequence, we failed to see that what we were doing degraded all of us. ...

When we see improvement, when we see more dignity, more confidence, more happiness—we will know we are going to win. We need these practical building blocks of change."

Redfern, Sydney, Australia 1992

Black and white equality in South Africa

The ex-South African president, Nelson Mandela has spent his life fighting for equal rights for black Africans. He gave this speech when he was on trial as leader of the African National Congress (ANC). He spent 27 years in prison for his beliefs, before becoming South Africa's first democratically-elected president in 1994.

"Above all, we want equal political rights, because without them our disabilities will be permanent.

... Their [the ANC's]struggle is a truly national one. It is a struggle of the African people, inspired by their own suffering and their own experience. It is a struggle for the right to live.

During my lifetime I have dedicated myself to this struggle of the African people. I have fought against white domination, and I have fought against black domination. I have cherished the ideal of a democratic and free society in which all persons live together in harmony and with equal opportunities. It is an ideal which I hope to live for and to achieve. But if needs be, it is an ideal for which I am prepared to die."

April 20, 1964

The injustice of slavery

Frederick Douglass was born as a slave in the United States in 1817, but escaped to freedom in 1838. He became a leader in the antislavery movement. In 1852 he was asked to give a speech as part of an Independence Day celebration. His speech was a shocking attack on slavery.

"There is not a man beneath the canopy of heaven who does not know that slavery is wrong for him. …

What to the American slave is your Fourth of July? I answer, a day that reveals to him more than all other days of the year, the gross injustice and cruelty to which he is the constant victim. To him your celebration is a sham; your boasted liberty an unholy license; your national greatness, swelling vanity; your sounds of rejoicing are empty and heartless; your shouts of liberty and equality, hollow mockery; your prayers and hymns, your sermons and thanksgivings, with all your religious parade and solemnity, are to him mere **bombast**, fraud, deception, **impiety**, and **hypocrisy**—a thin veil to cover up crimes which would disgrace a nation of savages. There is not a nation of the Earth guilty of practices more shocking and bloody than are the people of these United States at this very hour."

July 4, 1852

Voting rights for women

Women were not given the right to vote until fairly recently in most countries. Emmeline Pankhurst was a famous British **suffragette**, someone who fought for women's votes. She was jailed over and over again for it. In between jail sentences in 1913 she visited Hartford, Connecticut. She talked about how suffragettes were using every kind of publicity and disruption they could to make their point.

"You have two babies very hungry and wanting to be fed. One baby is a patient baby, and waits ... until its mother is ready to feed it. The other baby is an impatient baby and cries lustily, screams and kicks and makes everybody unpleasant until it is fed. Well, we know perfectly well which baby is attended to first.

That is the whole history of politics. You have to make more noise than anybody else, you have to make yourself more obtrusive [noticeable] than anybody else, ... in fact you have to be there all the time and see that they do not snow you under.

...We [women] wear no mark; we belong to every class ... of the community from the highest to the lowest; and so you see in the woman's civil war, the dear men of my country are discovering it is absolutely impossible to deal with it: you cannot locate it, and you cannot stop it."

November 13, 1913

29

Effective Visual Aids

Why use anything other than your voice to help add punch to your presentation? There are many reasons, but the most persuasive one is that many people remember what they see more clearly than what they hear or read.

PROPS AND VISUALS

Visual aids can emphasize important points. They can focus attention and change the mood in a room. Also, people like to look at things that move. Our brains have a hard time focusing on stillness. By giving your audience different things to see, you will keep bringing their attention back to your message.

Remember to keep props to a minimum. You don't want to distract your audience. Any props should be chosen carefully to enhance the content of your speech.

Simple illustrations will require the audience to listen to you for an explanation. That's good—you and your visual work together to increase the audience's understanding. Don't bring props that require elaborate explanations—unless, of course, that is what your speech is about.

TIP

When using any visual aid with words—such as posters, PowerPoint presentations, or slide shows—don't stop your presentation and read word for word what is being shown. Not everyone likes being read to. Also, it sounds stilted. But don't include too many words on your visuals—people will stop listening to you, and start reading. Let the words make short points that sit alongside your main talk and add to it. Cartoons and funny drawings with a few words are great. So are slides with three points you can use as headings to start you off.

Some ideas for props and visual aids you could use.	
Topic	**Visual aid**
Local government	Map of civic center offices
Why slavery is immoral	Picture of slaves packed into slave ship
What plants are best for your garden	Slide show of suitable plants; planting diagram
Why the voting age should be lowered to 16	Slide show of 16-17 year olds at work in "grown-up" professions such as catering

 Remember that handling awkward visual aids may be distracting for your audience.

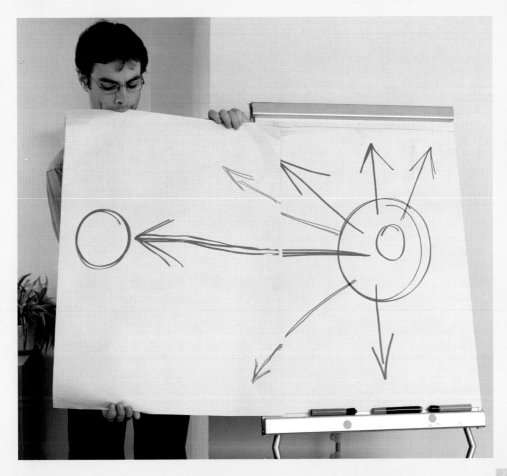

Get to Know the Venue

Next, you will need to know where and when the presentation will be given. Be sure to check out the room before you give your presentation. Nothing makes for great theater like the presenter tripping over cords, knocking things down, or finding something embarrassing written on a chalkboard. Make sure none of this happens to you by walking it through before you start.

Check out the **acoustics**. If you need an amplifier and microphone, get one before you start. It's easy to lose an audience that can't hear you.

Technology

Carefully inspect any technology you will be using—including light bulbs, microphones, speakers, and power cords—before your presentation. Don't just walk in and expect everything to be set up perfectly. Odds are it won't be. Don't just check the items listed. Think outside the box. If it can go wrong, it probably will.

If you are using a computer, make sure you have all of the extension cords, converters, cables, disks, and anything else you might need. If you are using someone else's computer, beware—check you won't be projecting an embarrassing desktop or screen saver to your audience.

Don't just rehearse your speech—rehearse your presentation. There is nothing more annoying than having to wait for someone to come fix your problem. It gets your performance off to a very bad start.

You'll feel more confident if you check out the place where you are speaking before your presentation. Check the equipment and get a feel for the space.

• CHECKLIST •

Follow this checklist to become a smooth presenter.

- Check all technology before the big presentation.

- Make sure any moving parts are working.

- Make sure light bulbs are functioning.

- Make sure microphones are working and sound good.

- Check that speakers are not blown out and are loud enough.

- Check that the computer will not shut down and that all the programs you need are loaded and running.

- If a presentation is saved onto a disk, be sure it is saved properly.

- If you need an easel, display space, or blue tack to display your visuals up with, check these will hold your visual aids without them falling down.

- Make sure you know the order of your visual presentations by heart.

PROPS AND VISUALS

1) Concerning props, you should
   a) Go overboard
   b) Never check to make sure they are functioning
   c) Keep them to a minimum
   d) Never use them

2) When prepping before the presentation, you should
   a) Inspect everything beforehand
   b) Rock back and forth nervously
   c) Not worry—everything will work fine
   d) Write your notes on your hand

3) Before your presentation you should be sure to
   a) Check out the room or venue
   b) Stay up the entire night
   c) Not worry about anything
   d) Get as many props as possible

Check page 50 to check your answers.

Practice Makes Perfect

You can do all the research, write a beautiful speech, and wear the perfect clothing, but unless you actually practice speaking, you will never get it perfect. Practice gives you the chance to see how your presentation can be improved before you do it "live."

Use Friends and Family

Start by practicing in front of a mirror behind a locked door. This will give you a chance to practice facial expressions, hand gestures, and body movement. You can time yourself, too. Next practice in front of friends or family. Watch how they react to what you say and show them. Ask them for feedback.

A good way to do this is to ask for two good things about the speech, and two things that could be improved. Accept their feedback gracefully. Don't argue, but do ask for more information if you are not clear what they meant. Don't be discouraged by any criticism— remember that your friends and family have the best intentions and are working to help you.

Famous words

Most off-the-cuff, or impromptu speeches are actually well-rehearsed. The speaker may not memorize the words, but will probably have a few key phrases down pat. Also, he or she will know the topic and the facts very well.

Getting it Right

Babysitting presents a good opportunity to practice your performance. Young children can be an excellent audience, and they won't make you as nervous as your peers or family might. You could really go overboard with hand and facial gestures, emphasis, tone, and timing. You can practice reading a picture book with lots of dialogue in it. Make a different voice for each character and really exaggerate it as your read. You'll be amazed how even the most over-the-top exaggeration will seem just right to the kids.

- Take a deep breath before you begin your speech. Remember to breathe between sentences and long phrases. Also pause and breathe between paragraphs, topics, or cards.

- Don't let your eyes dart around the audience. Pick one person, talk to that person for a few phrases, then move to another person. Include the whole room, but slowly!

- Make yourself sound confident and you will begin to feel confident.

- The night before the presentation, give your speech in front of your parents or friends, and ask for feedback.

- Take opportunities to speak in class. Each time you stand up in front of people and talk you gain valuable experience and lose some of your nerves. Soon, it starts to feel natural.

Giving your speech in front of young children will give you good practice in keeping an audience's attention!

VERBAL SKILLS

What are you looking to improve as you practice? This depends on where your strengths and weaknesses were when you began. One challenge most presenters face is keeping the audience listening. This is perhaps the most important thing you can do. Here are some ways to develop your speaking skills.

Speaking well

The first thing to keep in mind is volume. Many beginning speakers are either too soft or too loud. You need to have the appropriate volume for the room. One way to practice this is to have a friend move around the room to see if you are too loud or too soft as you speak.

Speed or rate is another concern. When people are nervous, they tend to speak quickly. Often novice speakers speak so quickly that no one can possibly take in what they are trying to say.

One way to slow yourself is to stop speaking when you are looking down—in other words, don't speak when you look at your notes. This will cause you to pause, which is not a bad thing. A pause after a good point will make it more effective. You can also put reminders in your notes to slow down or breathe.

Getting it Right

If you need help with pronunciation, you can practice with tongue twisters. Here are some to try:

- Is this your sister's sixth zither, sir?

- The sixth sick sheik's sixth sheep's sick.

- Three free throws.

- Lesser leather never weathered wetter weather better.

- How can a clam cram in a clean cream can?

- Seventy seven benevolent elephants

Pronunciation can be a problem for many public speakers. When speaking, you need to make sure that your audience can understand every word you're saying. One way to practice this is to exaggerate your lip movements. Slow down your speech and actually say each part of each word.

Stressing words

Which words should you place emphasis, or stress, on? Using the proper emphasis is critical in public speaking. Pausing before or after a word or phrase can show emphasis. The worst thing to do is to bore your audience. Speaking in a **monotone** voice will do this. In a few cases, audiences have even fallen asleep! Your audience will never hear what you have to say if you are uninteresting. This can be fixed with **inflections** which you can use to make your voice louder and stronger on important points or things that you feel are outrageous. Then you can lower the tone of your voice for sad, or shameful points.

Practice pronunciation by watching yourself speak in the mirror.

Choosing words

Word choice is a critical part of your delivery. Don't use the same words to describe everything in your speech. Watch some television commercials to find persuasive words and phrases.

Also, remember that public speaking is usually done in a formal setting. You need to use proper English, not the same language you use among your friends. Often we speak in slang, or use specialized words that not everyone can understand. Think of some examples. What words are commonly used by your friends that wouldn't be appropriate to say in front of your parents? What words would they not understand?

Remember your audience

Think of your whole audience, from oldest to youngest. Think of people who may not speak English as their first language. Remember to choose words they will all understand. If you use difficult or **specialized vocabulary**, define any difficult terms.

If you choose to use words that will shock your audience, know why you are using them and go carefully. If you are not sure whether what you want to say is appropriate, ask a teacher, parent, or librarian and explain what you are trying to achieve.

Getting it Wrong

"**Amandas**" are a common problem with all speakers. These are filler words, such as "um" and "uh." Often people use filler words when thinking out loud, as they try to find the correct word or thought.

Other Amandas are "you know," "like," "well . . . ," "anyway," "okay," "yeah," "right"—and many, many others. Sometimes it is just a really deep sigh.

Almost every single person uses Amandas in everyday speech—and we mostly don't even notice we are doing it. However, they become more noticeable when someone is speaking publicly, and can be distracting and annoying for an audience. Listen to yourself speaking— you could even record yourself—and count how many Amandas you utter in a minute. Then try to cure yourself of the Amanda habit!

Getting rid of fillers

A good way to rid yourself of filler words is by practicing a one-minute speech. This practice consists of a speaker, and a judge with a bell and a timer. The speaker must stand and speak for one entire minute without using any Amandas or long pauses, and without repeating himself or herself or going off topic. If the speaker breaks any of the rules, the judge rings a bell. The speaker loses that round. Then the judge sets the timer again, and starts over with a new topic.

It might sound easy, but it is quite tricky and tests your skills. It also can be a lot of fun, especially if you make it a group activity.

DID YOU KNOW?

Cicero (below, center) was a great Roman speaker who lived more than 2,000 years ago. He had many thoughts on public speaking. He said that **orators** should have a wide knowledge so their speeches will include beauty and fullness. He believed in natural talent, and said great speakers have the ability to invent, talk a lot, and speak strongly in interesting tones. They look pleasant. They stay human—using their passion and enthusiasm to convince the audience. More than 2,000 years later, these things are still true!

NONVERBAL SKILLS

People don't just listen to your words and look at your visual aids. They also follow your **nonverbal** cues. You give lots of these without even knowing it. Some of the biggies are:

- Where you look
- How you stand or move around
- What you do with your hands
- Your **posture**

If you can get your nonverbal cues to match up with everything else you do, you will be a very convincing speaker. Your presentation will succeed in holding the audience's attention, informing them, and hopefully persuading them to take your view.

Where you look

Proper eye contact is hard for a beginning speaker. It is perhaps the most important nonverbal skill to master. If you are trying to keep an audience interested, eye contact is critical. Look around the room—don't just focus on one spot.

Good and frequent eye contact with the audience will also help with your speaking speed. If you make yourself look around, you will slow down. Don't let your eyes dart around, however. And remember, don't speak when looking at your notes.

How you stand

Try to refrain from distracting motions. When you stand up to speak, don't move around. Plant your feet firmly so you don't rock back and forth or keep stepping back and then forward. If you need to move during the presentation, take decisive steps and plant yourself firmly again when you get where you're going. Don't dance around.

What you do with your hands

Part of success is knowing your faults. If you know you play with your hair when you're nervous, be sure to tie it back. If you like to adjust the speaker's stand throughout your speech, try to keep your hands off it.

Some hand movements make you appear fidgety, nervous, or unprepared. You want to remain credible in the minds of audience members, so stay professional. During practice, ask your test audience to point out any annoying habits.

Proper eye contact and hand gestures will help to keep your audience's attention. Try not to overuse one gesture, or stare at one person for too long.

Hand gestures can make a speech more intriguing. However, this does not mean you should wave your hands all over the place during the entire speech. One strong gesture involves making a fist and pounding the bottom of it into your other outstretched hand. Use this gesture when you are saying something important that you want to make sure the audience hears. You can also match words with gestures. For example, if you are saying "Our plan will make these problems go away," you can sweep your hand in front of you on the word "away." Hand motions are powerful as long as they are not overused.

STAND UP STRAIGHT!

Great speakers have **poise**, which means they stand up straight and look confident. Professional voice trainers focus a lot on how you stand. Good posture will help you with breathing, pronunciation, eye contact, and volume.

If you slump, you can't fill your lungs up properly. Without a good air supply, your voice can't project or last very long. You also get tired more quickly, because your muscles are not working with your skeleton to hold you upright. They are using a lot of effort just to keep you slumped.

Sooner or later you'll probably end up with back pain and shoulder pain if you keep slumping. So, let's fix your posture. You'll need a full-length mirror to help.

Stand up and follow the exercises on the right (1 through 6). Do you now look more balanced and even? Try this again, turned sideways to the mirror. Go through the standing up straight process, then turn your head to look at your body from the side. You should be able to draw an imaginary line from the crown of your head through the shoulders, hips, knees and feet just in front of the ankles. Can you? Are you leaning back or forward? If you are, try rocking on your feet until you are not leaning.

4

As you tucked your tailbone in, did your chest lift? That's what you want to feel—like your breastbone is reaching up to give your lungs space to fill.

3

Next, look at your hips. Are they directly under your shoulders? Move them so they are not in front, behind, or off to one side. They should also be level, so you feel your tailbone tucking in slightly.

2

Let your knees be slightly loose, so you feel springy.

1

Begin by taking off your shoes and looking in the mirror as you stand normally. Now focus on your feet. Take them about a foot (30 cm) apart. Rock onto the toes and back onto the heels. Do this until you can balance between the toes and heels, over the arches of the feet.

5

Stretch the back of your neck so it lengthens. Lift the crown, or very top of your head, up to the sky. Your head should float above your neck. You may feel slightly taller, like your spine is growing up to the ceiling.

6

Now look at your shoulders. Slide the shoulder blades down your back towards your waist. Focus on dropping hunched shoulder muscles away from your ears.

Well balanced

When you master standing up straight, pause. Memorize how this feels, so you can do it again without a mirror. Practice standing up straight whenever you can, and your muscles will soon learn to hold you in this posture naturally.

Now when you speak, your lungs can fill with air and fuel your speech. You won't move around while speaking because you are firmly balanced on the ground. And it won't hurt to stand for a long time, because your body is well balanced.

Getting it Wrong

How do you know if you've lost your audience? If their nonverbal cues tell you! For instance, they:

• Look down a lot
• Rub their faces or hair
• Fidget and yawn, or even sigh
• Look through notes
• Lean back in their chairs and look up
• Cross their arms
• Tap their feet.

Try startling them back to join you—make a noise, drop a book. Then be engaging and win them back over.

Read your audience's nonverbal signs so you know when you need to try harder to keep them interested.

Mastering the skills

It will take a lot of practice and a lot of time to master these skills. Research has shown that if you say something confident and positive, but your body language says you feel shy or nervous, your audience is less likely to believe in you. Make sure your voice, body language, and nonverbal cues are strong and positive, and your speech will be a success.

Distractions

Be sure to keep distractions to a minimum. They can turn a fantastic and well-thought-out speech into a disastrous one. For instance, if you have a habit of clicking your pen, put it away. If you stand up with it, you could be tempted to keep clicking it. If you know that you fiddle with your hair when you're feeling nervous, tie it back. Fidgeting actions will take the audience's attention off your speech and put it on your clicking pen—or increasingly rumpled hair!

SPEAKING SKILLS

1) **When getting feedback on your speech, it is important to:**
   a) Get angry.
   b) Not become discouraged.
   c) Keep in mind that most people don't know what they are talking about.
   d) None of the above.

2) **One way to slow down is to:**
   a) Read word for word.
   b) Not bring any notes so you have to make yourself remember.
   c) Not speak when you look down.
   d) Pause to bite your nails.

3) **Proper eye contact is important because:**
   a) If you don't, the audience may leave.
   b) It helps to keep an audience interested.
   c) You can scare your audience.
   d) You can wink at your friends.

Check page 50 to check your answers.

TIP

Even the best speakers sometimes forget to breathe. You can even put reminders to do this in your notes. Try labeling notecards with the words "BREATHE!" or "SLOW DOWN!"

Bringing It All Together

So, you are full of knowledge and enthusiasm you want to share. You have written and practiced a brilliant speech. You have good visual aids to add information and interest. But you're still nervous? Here are some ideas to help you.

Beating Nerves

People suffer different kinds of nervousness. Shaking, feeling sick, needing the toilet, whispering, giggling, going very still—all these are normal. You can control them!

Even the most experienced presenters get nervous before a speech. A little nervousness brings focus to your presentation, and sharpens your mind. Mark Twain said, "There are two types of speakers, those that are nervous and those that are liars."

Being too relaxed can work against you. So just rein in those nerves and let them go when you start. Be totally in the moment when you begin, without fear. You will be great!

What to wear

Dress appropriately! This is harder than it sounds. It is important not to underdress or overdress. Make it correct for your audience and your topic. Remember to be comfortable, though. It's not a good time to wear new shoes or anything too tight. If you feel comfortable, you are less likely to be nervous.

Getting it Wrong

If you look like you fell into your younger sister's costume box, your audience could be distracted by your many props and not take you as seriously as they would if you had one or two effective props. For example, if you are making a presentation about fairytales and constantly waving around a magic wand, your audience will follow the wand instead of what you are saying.

If your speech is about going to Hawaii, dress for it. Getting the clothing correct can make the presentation. However, be sure the costume or whatever you are wearing is not so distracting that the audience loses focus on the main topic.

A silly costume will make an audience laugh, but make sure that's not the only thing that stays in their minds!

Interruptions

Most audiences are happy to listen to you politely. If you are interesting and enthusiastic, they will listen intently. Sometimes someone will interrupt you. What do you do?

- Don't panic. You know your subject. If it's a question that just can't wait, answer it. If it can wait, say "I'll be getting to that in just a minute." If you don't know the answer, say "That's a great question. I'll have to look up the answer later. Can we talk after the presentation?"

- If the interruption is rude, don't get flustered. Ask politely for the person to wait and talk to you after the presentation. If someone is really rude or disruptive, you can ask him or her to leave.

- If the interruption is not by choice —someone is sick, a fire drill, a chair falling over—you need to gauge the mood. Take care of the problem, then begin again from where you left off. If it seems like the right thing to do, you can say something like, "Don't you hate it when that happens?" or "Thanks for bearing with me while we sorted that out."

What if it all goes wrong?

Sometimes things go wrong. The power is cut, your visuals disappear, your notes dissolve. Whatever happens, it seems designed to ruin your presentation. However, if you know your subject and have practiced well, you can rise above most disasters.

Acknowledge the problem. Apologize briefly if appropriate. Then move on. If you have to, abandon the prepared speech and just tell your audience what you want them to know.

Don't try to describe lost or ruined visuals. Just forget about them. Stop thinking about what you were going to do, take stock, and just do what you can to the best of your ability. Remember, the audience does not know what you have prepared. The audience only know what you tell them. Don't tell them what you had intended to do. Dazzle them with your knowledge instead.

And when you've finished …

Be sure to reflect on your presentation. Write down what you did well and what you can do better. Next time you can build on your strengths. And take time to congratulate yourself on your achievement. You did it!

Finish your presentation on a high note. Wrap things up strongly or end with a flourish your audience will remember.

• CHECKLIST •

Here are some ways to relax before your presentation:

- Close your eyes and breathe in and out steadily. Without forcing it, make the exhale longer than the inhale. Don't breathe any deeper than normal, simply make the out breath last longer.

- Singing cures stutters and bad posture. It helps you breathe well, too. Practice by singing anything you like, but make it fairly loud!

- Lie down and be comfortable and still. Let your body relax. Breathe deeply. Think about each part of your body from your feet to your head and relax each part.

- Avoid sugar or caffeine before a presentation. Bring a glass of water with you and if your mouth feels dry, take a sip.

"There are always three speeches for every one you actually gave: the one you practiced, the one you gave, and the one you wish you gave."

–Dale Carnegie (1888–1955), American writer and lecturer

QUIZ

PUTTING IT ALL TOGETHER

1) **You should remind yourself to**
   a) Breathe
   b) Say "*um*" and "*uh*"
   c) Laugh nervously
   d) Eat

2) **When dressing for your speech, you should**
   a) Roll out of bed and go
   b) Not worry about it
   c) Dress as if you are going to prom
   d) Dress appropriately for your topic and audience

3) **Once the speech is made, you should**
   a) Run around jumping with joy and screaming
   b) Sleep
   c) Do nothing
   d) Identify what you can do better next time

Check page 50 to check your answers.

QUIZ RESULTS

TEST YOUR PROGRESS
For page 9

1) d)

2) a)

3) d)

PROPS AND VISUAL AIDS
For page 33

1) c)

2) a)

3) a)

BEGINNING RESEARCH
For page 15

1) a)

2) d)

3) d)

SPEAKING SKILLS
For page 45

1) b)

2) c)

3) b)

SPEECH DELIVERY
For page 25

1) a)

2) c)

3) a)

PUTTING IT ALL TOGETHER
For page 49

1) a)

2) d)

3) d)

(20) Things To Remember

1 Know your subject inside and out!

2 Give yourself time to do your research well. Use a variety of resources to help with your research.

3 Build your speech around a framework of facts.

4 Listen to great speeches to hear how other people have used words—what do you like? Why? Use this information to help you write a great speech.

5 Learn to stand well. Good posture helps you feel confident, speak well and stay steady.

6 Use your voice to its full ability. Vary your tone. Be heard.

7 Choose your words well—leave your Amandas at home.

8 Use notecards instead of writing the whole speech out. You'll sound more natural.

9 Pick visuals that add to your presentation. Don't repeat what you say with your visual aids.

10 Keep it simple.

11 Calm your nerves by breathing steadily, with focus. Make your exhale (outward breath) longer than your inhale (inward breath). This will calm you down.

12 Practice, practice, practice.

13 Ask for feedback—from your practice audience, and from people after you give your presentation. Use it to help be better next time.

14 Dress well. Be neat and tidy, or costumed, but think it all through beforehand.

15 Check out the room before a speech or presentation. Make sure all the technology is working.

16 Don't panic if things go wrong. Fix the problem, take a breath, and begin again.

17 Slow down! Breathe!

18 Make eye contact with the audience, one person at a time, and go slowly.

19 Bring nothing with you that will distract you from your presentation.

20 Believe in yourself!

Further Information

BOOKS

California High School Association's Curriculum Committee. *Speaking Across the Curriculum: Practical Ideas for Incorporating Listening and Speaking into the Classroom*. New York: International Debate Education Association, 2004.

Marrs, Carol and Lafe Locke. *The Complete Book of Speech Communication: A Workbook of Ideas and Activities for Students of Speech and Theatre*. Colorado Springs: Meriwether Publishing, 1992.

Meany, John and Kate Shuster. *Speak Out! Debate and Public Speaking in the Middle Grades*. New York: International Debate Education Association, 2005.

Schloff, Laurie and Marcia Yudkin. *Smart Speaking: 60-Second Strategies for More Than 100 Speaking Problems and Fears (Audio Cassette)*. New York: Blue Penguin Publications, 1993.

WEBSITES

Websites with speeches featured in this book:

Dr. Martin Luther King Jr., "I Have a Dream," page 7
www.americanrhetoric.com/speeches/mlkihaveadream.htm

John F. Kennedy, "We choose to go to the Moon" page 13
www.historyplace.com/speeches/jfk-space.htm

Patrick Henry, "Liberty or Death," page 21
www.historyplace.com/speeches/henry.htm
Richard Schumann reading the speech (he plays Patrick Henry at Colonial Williamsburg)
www.history.org/Almanack/people/bios/biohen.cfm#speech

Winston Churchill, "We Shall Fight on the Beaches," page 23
www.winstonchurchill.org/i4a/pages/index.cfm?pageid=393

Paul Keating's speech, page 26
www.antar.org.au/content/view/24/1/

Nelson Mandela, "I am Prepared to Die," page 27
www.anc.org.za/ancdocs/history/rivonia.html

Frederick Douglass, "The Meaning of July Fourth for the Negro," page 28
www.pbs.org/wgbh/aia/part4/4h2927t.html

Emmeline Pankhurst, "Freedom or death," page 29
www.guardian.co.uk/greatspeeches/story/0,,2059295,00.html

Other websites with great speeches:

www.history.com/media.do

www.learnoutloud.com/Catalog/History

www.americanrhetoric.com/top100speechesall.html

www.school-for-champions.com/speeches.htm

Useful websites with tips for public speaking, speech writing, and speaking exercises:

www.write-out-loud.com/dictionexercises.html

Exercises to help you speak more clearly.

www.dictionary.com

Check any specialized words you use to make sure you understand them fully.

www. school-for-champions.com/speaking.htm

Good tips for public speaking.

Glossary

acoustics size or characteristics of a location that determine sound quality

alliteration when the sounds in a group of words are the same—all beginning with the letter "b," for example

Amandas filler words used during speaking, such as "um" and "uh"

bombast high language with little meaning

civil rights person's rights as guaranteed by the U.S. Constitution

conviction being sure about a topic, speaking with authority on a topic

discrimination excluding a person or people, often because of their race

emotive stirring up emotion

emphasis use of pitch or tone to stress a word or phrase

eye contact act of looking directly into another person's eyes

hypocrisy pretending to have certain qualities

impiety having no respect or regard for religious values

impromptu done without preparation

indigenous originating from a particular place

inflections adding or reducing volume as you speak

monotone using only one tone

nonverbal communicated using the body, not the voice

orators public speakers that are especially highly skilled

Patriot colonist who rebelled against British control during the American Revolution

philosopher someone who studies to gain wisdom about the meaning of life

poise dignified, self-confident manner or bearing

posture the way in which a person holds their body, or a particular position in which someone stands

prejudice unfair treatment of a group of people who belong to a certain race or religion

pretentious trying to appear impressive or important

procrastination act of putting off doing something until the last minute

specialized vocabulary special terms used in a particular field

stilted stiff or unnatural

suffragette campaigner for votes for women when they were not allowed to vote

teleprompter device used in television to show a script to the person who is speaking

United Nations international organization that aims to maintain peace and stability in the world

visual aid something for the audience to look at, such as a slide show or PowerPoint presentation

Index

CRABAPPLE
MIDDLE SCHOOL
MEDIA CENTER